ALSO BY BRADLEY HARTMANN

THE SKEPTICAL LUMBERMAN
Guide to Social Media

GOOD TO EXCELENTE
How Excellent Companies Embrace Hispanic Cultural
Differences to Improve Productivity, Safety, Retention,
and Sales

BEHIND YOUR BACK

BEHIND YOUR BACK

What purchasing managers say once you leave the room and how to get them to say yes.

by

Bradley Hartmann

Behind Your Back Sales Co. | Dallas, TX

Hartmann, Bradley.
Behind Your Back:
What purchasing managers say once you leave the
room and how to get them to say yes.

Designed in the United States of America.

behindyourbacksales.com

1 2 3 4 5 6 7 8 9

SECOND EDITION

Book design by Jason Hines
nicehines.com

For Will,
the toughest kid I know.

Lack of candor basically blocks smart ideas, fast action, and good people contributing all the stuff they've got.

It's a killer.

—Jack Welch

CONTENTS

INTRODUCTION

THE STORY BEHIND
BEHIND YOUR BACK

From 2007 to 2011, I was a Midwest area purchasing manager at Pulte Homes, one of the largest homebuilders in the nation. Based in suburban Chicago, I bought materials and labor for thousands of homes built under the Pulte, Del Webb, and Centex brands constructed in the Midwest from Cleveland, Ohio, to Denver, Colorado.

I worked with dozens of subcontractors and suppliers of all shapes and sizes and learned a great deal about products, pricing, and presentations, but it always came back to the people. The variety of people made the work fascinating, it made my job fun.

OK . . . the *good ones* did.
The people who were good at their jobs made my job fun. They made purchasing enjoyable—and they made it easy.

They made my life easy.
They made saying *yes* easy.
They made negotiating easy.
They made change orders easy.

They *got* it.

One afternoon, I was telling a teammate about one such salesman. This guy was sharp. He was articulate. He was insightful. And after each meeting, he would send a handwritten note—a quick thanks along with the commitments he'd made during the meeting. This gesture alone was rather unique, but what was even more impressive was how quickly he'd send them. His cards were always postmarked the same day as our meeting. Always.

This guy was different.
No one else I knew sent handwritten notes.[1]

It was memorable.

It was a lesson about what you *should do*.

Then my teammate countered with an equally memorable story—about a train wreck of a subcontractor.

It was a story about *what you shouldn't do.*

We exchanged these stories—the good and the bad—daily.

So we eventually drafted a list consisting of two categories:
1. What reps did to help them win business
2. What reps did that caused them to lose business

We joked about providing this list of do's and don'ts to anyone seeking a meeting with us. It would serve as a guide book to winning our business.

---

1. Handwritten notes will never go out of style. Just make sure you don't have the penmanship of a six-year-old. That won't help you.

Want a meeting to pitch me on your new insulation business? Absolutely! Just read this first and call me in 30 days.

The list would save us time.
The list would save them time.

This book is that list.

HOW TO USE THIS BOOK

You'll notice the 48 recommendations that make up the four parts of this book are brief. Resist the temptation to rip through 20 of them during one trip to the corporate loo.

This isn't a speed-reading contest.
Take them one at a time.

Attempt to do what the book actually recommends you do.

At your next sales meeting, pick out one item and spend 15 minutes discussing it candidly as a team.

If your team's consensus differs from mine, that's entirely possible. Your mileage may vary.

The validation of your thought process and your commitment to improvement will come in the form of new business.

Start where the pain is the worst.
Keep an open mind.

Here's a short list of questions we'll answer in this book:

- *What's the one question I need to be ready to answer?*
- *What's the guaranteed way to get my phone call returned?*
- *How can I handle the "transparency" demand effectively?*
- *Should I believe the guy when he says I'm 2 percent high on my bid?*
- *How do I relate to a purchasing manager when I have shoes that are older than he is?*

This book is divided into four parts. These represent the path to turning a suspect into a prospect and then a prospect into a customer.[2]

1. Achieving Awareness
2. Mastering the Meeting
3. Navigating the Negotiation
4. Amazing Your Account

Each part contains 12 recommendations.

If my math is right, that's a total of 48 rules to live by. About one per week for a year—excluding holidays, vacation days, and the day you're hungover after the Super Bowl.

The best news?

None of this will blow your mind.

The things on this list aren't harebrained schemes. They're basic, straightforward ideas—and you can start doing them immediately. On behalf of purchasing managers everywhere, *we wish you would!*

Here is my promise: If executed consistently and thoughtfully, this list will win you more business.

This list documents how some of the best salespeople I've ever met won new business. I am confident it will do the same for you.

Oh, and one more thing.

I know what you're thinking.
You're thinking about the *p* word: *price.*

---

2. I stole this from Zig Ziglar. Not sure whom he stole it from . . .

Nowhere in the following pages will you find any mandate about needing to have the lowest price. If you do have the lowest price, hey—that'll surely be helpful. But it's not necessary.

Good purchasing managers know the real price to be paid when the wrong subcontractor or supplier is chosen. They understand the "total cost of ownership."

Frustration.
Change Orders.
Backordered material.
Angry superintendents.
Endless conference calls.

In short, a ton of rework.

Purchasing managers want to avoid this.

The need for competitive pricing is a given—you at least need to be in the ballpark. But having the lowest price is not a requirement; it's merely one element in the overall buying decision. What's more important is understanding all of the factors at play, and this book will help you do just that.

Now let's get to work.

ACHIEVING AWARENESS

In Part I—Achieving Awareness—we'll discuss the best techniques to ensure you land on your prospect's radar—as a sharp, insightful expert who always delivers value first.

RULE 1.1

START WITH WHY

Why, exactly, are you pursuing this business—
MY business?

If you don't know . . . stop.

Stop what you're doing and think about why you want
this work. Be specific.

What do you know about my company?

How do we treat our employees?
How do we treat our suppliers?

Do we train our people?
Do we have high turnover?

Each one of these questions can have a big impact on
your ability to succeed at your job and enjoy doing it.

Big companies are like big dogs: they are hard to
control and they produce more shit.

To ensure your target prospect is a good fit for your business, consider the fundamentals of speed, quality, and price—the prospect can pick any two.

Trade-offs must be made.
Prospects can't choose all three.

If your prospect cares only about price and speed, and your firm has built a reputation for the highest quality, you and your prospect may not be the best fit.

If your prospect cares only about price, then that's an easy decision. Move on. An account won by a dollar will soon be lost by a dollar.

Start with why.
Carefully think through what you want and why you want it.

Because as the saying goes, "Be careful what you wish for. You just might get it."

RULE 1.2

GORDON GEKKO'S
2ND PRINCIPLE

You know Gordon Gekko's first principle:
Greed is good.

But the *Wall Street* antagonist's second principle is
more important to knowing how to win new business
without making your gross margins disappear.

In the film, Gekko asks his protégé, Bud Fox, a leading
question, to which we should all answer Yes!

*"The most valuable commodity I know of is
information. Wouldn't you agree?"*

Information is especially critical in the early stages
of a business relationship. The more you know about
your prospect, the better.

A supplier looking for an opportunity to bid our

work used his information well. In our first call, he casually mentioned something about his beloved Iowa Hawkeyes. Being a University of Illinois alum, I replied with some cheap shot, probably involving corn.

Some witty banter ensued about Big Ten football. He then mentioned his experience in the Chicago market.

Hey! I live in Chicago!

Some chatting about the Windy City led to a conversation about growing up watching Michael Jordan, the Bulls, and their six championships.

I thought to myself, *I could do this all day* . . .
And I nearly did.

Before I knew it, we had talked for an hour.
This wasn't pure coincidence.

He had done his homework. He had plenty of material to get a conversation rolling.

I hadn't seen any pricing from him yet, but I knew I liked him. He was authentic.

The references he made to my bio were inserted into our conversation effortlessly. It wasn't forced.[3]

The result of our first call was simple: *I could imagine us working together*. And when you are in prospecting mode, this achievement in a single call is a victory.

"The most valuable commodity I know of is information. Wouldn't you agree?"

---

3. Be careful here. Knowing someone's alma mater doesn't mean much if you can't weave it into the conversation with ease. Be authentic. Be real. Always.

RULE 1.3

GOOGLE US

Go to google.com.
Enter your name.

What comes up?

Is it good?
Is it bad?

Is it . . . nothing?

Enter your company's name.

What comes up?

Is it good?
Is it bad?

Is it . . . nothing?

Some Google algorithm doesn't control the content of

what shows up when someone searches your name—
you do.[4] Make sure when someone Googles you, they
find something positive about you.

Now . . . Google me.
(Not *me* really . . . your prospect.)

What do you find?
Dig in.

Find out everything you can.

Schedule a 15-minute block of time to research your
prospect.

Remember: the door swings both ways. You can be
sure I will have Googled you and your company prior
to our meeting. Be prepared to answer any questions
that may surface from your Google search results.

If you drove your car into a lake last New Year's Eve—
you better be prepared to share one heck of a story.

Quick Recap:
  Step Uno: Google me.
  Step Dos: Google you.

---

4. My editor pointed out that a Google algorithm does in fact determine your
   search results. And he's correct. My point is that you don't have to be a
   passive observer. You can influence what Google finds by being active and
   helpful online.

RULE 1.4

SCREW THE IT DEPARTMENT

Whenever someone new reaches out to me, I always investigate the person and his or her company. Google for the company (see Rule 1.3: "Google Us.") and LinkedIn for the person (Rule 1.6 is coming up shortly).

Every time.

Eventually I land on the website of the company the person works for. The information on there matters to me. It says something about the company and it indicates a certain level of thinking about your customers.

Why did I come to your website?
What answers am I searching for?

If you believe your people are your biggest asset . . .

If you believe your people represent your biggest competitive advantage . . .

Then put them on your website. If the IT department is too busy with other things, screw 'em. Find someone else to do it.

I'm already curious about the guy who's been calling me. That's why I'm visiting your site.

Tell me about your biggest asset. Brag to me about your competitive advantage. Don't bury the lead. Make the headline compelling and make the point obvious.

Bottom Line: Take control of your website—it's an important sales tool. Make sure it helps drive new leads and new sales.

Yeah, I know there are plenty of excuses.
And I don't care if your IT guy is cranky.

Do it anyway.

NFL teams have 53 players.
All their stats are updated weekly.

How is this relevant?

Like the NFL, you are in the talent business.
Show it off.

You know what I care about?
The talent in your company.

Why?

Because in order for me to succeed at my job, you—and your team—need to succeed at *your* job.

Your website can be an incredible sales tool, but it can't be left up to non-salespeople to figure it out.

Screw the IT department.

Take over the website and make sure it actually helps you sell.

RULE 1.5

BE LIKE THE BIEBS

Facebook.[5]
Twitter.[6]
LinkedIn.[7]
Instagram.[8]
Houzz.[9]

You don't have to love them.
You don't even have to use them.

But you do need to have a general understanding
of what they are. Don't stick your head in the sand
and hope it all goes away. Be like Justin Bieber—*The
Biebs*—embrace Millennials with flaming thumbs
a-flitter.

---

5. facebook.com
6. twitter.com
7. linkedin.com
8. instagram.com
9. houzz.com

If the name Justin Bieber eludes you, he's the pop sensation who exploded onto the music scene as a 13-year-old after his mother posted his videos on Youtube.[10] More than a decade later, Bieber has built a brand and an empire by leveraging the power of social media.

Social media can—and does—impact business.

How much so?

It depends.
You know your market better than I do.

What I do know is that people enjoy pictures. And often they engage with them more naturally than they do with text. Pictures are worth a 1,000 words, I'm told.

And I know Facebook, Instagram, Twitter, and Houzz are great for sharing pictures—and ideas.

So how can these social-media platforms best serve your company?

You need to decide that.

The younger generation of purchasing managers grew up with these tools. Being clueless—or, worse yet, angry—about their existence will not help you.

So be curious.
Be informed.
Be current.

Ask yourself one question: *What would Bieber do?*

---

10. youtube.com

RULE 1.6

LINK UP, LINK IN

Are you on LinkedIn?

Do you have an updated profile on the professional-network website?

You should.
LinkedIn is a must.

You are who you hang around with (online and off).
If it appears you hang around with no one, I'll assume you are out of touch. Or creepy.

I try not to contract with creepy people.

After Googling your website, LinkedIn is the next place I go to learn about you.

Starting from scratch?

Build out your profile in brief.

Then join a group or two.
If there are no groups, start one.

Participate in discussions.
If there are no discussions, start one.

Invest 20 minutes a week establishing your
LinkedIn profile.

On LinkedIn, you'll be able to list where you live,
where you went to school, where you've worked, the
people who recommend you, the organizations you
belong to, content you've published, and the best way
to connect with you—online or off.

Each of these profile elements is a potential
touchpoint with a prospect.

The résumé is dead.
LinkedIn is now your résumé.

Once you've invested some time creating an
informative profile, invest another 20 minutes
researching your prospects.

It's a small industry we're in. Leverage the strong and
weak ties in your network for your benefit.

If you want to meet Tom Johnson at Johnson Homes,
see if you know anyone who knows Tom. Then have
that mutual friend make an introduction.

It's that easy: linkedin.com.[11]

---

11.   Yes, LinkedIn is a public company. No, I don't own any shares.

RULE 1.7

UNSUCK YOUR BUSINESS CARDS

Most business cards suck.

The vast majority of them are boring, lame, reek of corporate compromise, and are ultimately forgettable.

After collecting hundreds of business cards from all over the country, I remember exactly one. And I still have it.

A carpenter contractor from Chicago had his business cards printed on wood.

Wooden business cards.
For a carpenter.

Get it?

Not only was it an instant conversation starter whenever he handed it out, later it would come up around my office whenever we'd discuss contractors who were innovative.

Was this guy actually running an innovative business?
I don't know. He ran a solid carpentry company, not
Apple.

I do know, at least on this one aspect of marketing
his business, that he was thinking differently than
everyone else.

This was a great design choice for his company. If
and when I ever had an itch to scratch involving
carpenters, I'd go straight to my book of business
cards.

And guess which carpenter I'd think of first?

You got it.
Mr. Wooden Business Card.
He received top-of-mind status.

A few other notes on business cards:

PAPER PERFECT

Print yours on 100 lb. card stock. If you try to save a
few pennies per card by choosing the next step up
from toilet paper, we may confuse the two.

Why are these cards so cheap?
Or do they not know these are cheap?

What does the quality of their cards say about the
quality of their company? What does this say about
how they feel about us?

Is it possible I'm looking too far into this?
Maybe.

But I did and I still do.

DESIGN-DRIVEN

Don't be afraid to be original and interesting. Pay a few bucks to have a graphic designer create something unique. Something people will remember and mention after you leave.

Change them up every six months.

Have four different models of business cards with different products on the back. See which one your prospects like the best. Make a game out of it.

Business cards are cheap.
Have some fun with them.

My current business cards are transparent.
And plastic.

They cost $0.11 each.

And my title on these transparent, inexpensive business cards is *Recovering Purchasing Manager*.

Yes, really.
Recovering Purchasing Manager is on my business card.

I can tell you firsthand, having *Recovering Purchasing Manager* on a business card is a guaranteed conversation starter. And it's memorable. I've ran into people I met only once and they say, "Hey, it's the *Recovering Purchasing Manager*!"

Damn right.

DELIVERY DRIVERS

You have team members who visit your customers every day. For many of your customers, these colleagues of yours are quite literally the face of your brand.

Who are they?

Exactly. Your delivery drivers. If you believe the mantra that everyone is in sales (and you should—it's the truth), then arm these folks with business cards. Your delivery team is interacting with customers every single day and are probably an underutilized resource.

Ask your drivers what customers are saying about your products, your people, and your brand. They may have some truly valuable information—but you have to ask them first.

SPEAK SPANISH

If you have Spanish-speaking customers, get business cards in Spanish. Don't overthink this. Just do it.

Hispanics are the largest minority in the country and the most entrepreneurial ethnic group, and they will represent a significant source of your revenue—if they don't already.

Treat them with respect. Be different.

Business cards in Spanish will accomplish both.

RULE 1.8

SWING BY SALES

Sales drive the business.

As a young superintendent, I didn't appreciate this truth.

Especially when I was busting my ass, building and servicing dozens of homes each month. Not to mention making 80 percent less than our sales team.

But it's true.

Sales. Drive. The. Business.

Once 2007 hit and the go-go years of homebuilding were toast, everyone began praying at the SDTB[12] altar.

So . . . with this in mind, what should you do?

---

12. Sales drive the business. C'mon . . . stay with me here.

Talk to my salespeople.

Ask them which of your products could make their job easier.

Ask them which trends are most exciting to their prospects.

Don't overthink the process of engaging in a conversation with the sales team. Their job consists largely of waiting for someone to walk in the door.

Be that person.
Walk in that door and start gathering information.

If my sales team is buying what you're selling, I'm much more likely to buy also.

RULE 1.9

DELIVER VALUE FIRST

Persistence is a good substitute for talent, but persistently calling and requesting a meeting when you haven't provided anything of value is annoying.

Give me a reason to meet with you.

Spark my interest.
Share an insight.
Say something unexpected.
Show me something new.
Tell me a joke.

Do something.

Provide value first.

Now . . . what constitutes value?

Shortly after I landed in purchasing, one market had a pressing need for drywall negotiations.

We had two suppliers.
Both were average.

No one loved 'em.
No one hated 'em.

Being new in the position and short on time, I was told
to rollover the current contracts with both suppliers
and try to save a few bucks along the way.

Then I received a voicemail from a third supplier.

*"Hi Bradley, I heard you were new to the market
and wanted to introduce myself. We haven't worked
with Pulte yet, but we'd love the chance to make
your life easier. Your current suppliers have probably
mentioned it, but we expect a sizable decrease
in board prices next month. Also, I visited your
Carrington jobsite and counted 22 sheets of 1/2"
and 17 sheets of 5/8" sitting in the garages of five
completed homes—I have pictures I can send you, too.
I spoke to the installers and have some ideas about
where the extras are coming from. Talk to you soon."*

Impressive.

I liked this guy.
He provided a lot of value in a 20-second voicemail.

As for my current suppliers . . .

My current suppliers told me there was no room
for price decreases. *"Rumors of allocation from the
manufacturers . . ."*

Right.

My current suppliers told me their takeoffs were tight. *"There ain't one extra sheet anywhere on that job. I check everyday."*

Right.

With one voicemail, this mystery man was poised to land all of our drywall business. A few days later we connected for a call. He was insightful and straightforward.

"Feel free to ask me anything," he said. *"I'll shoot you straight and I never talk bad about my competitors. But . . . I have lots of ideas on how we can lower your costs, tighten up your takeoffs, and make you look really smart."*

A few weeks later he landed 100 percent of the business. And then he went out and did exactly what he said he would do.

That's providing value first.

Dropping off a folder with your company's information is not valuable.

It's recyclable.

RULE 1.10

OPEN A CURIOSITY GAP

Being in purchasing is like working for the IRS.

Whether you deserve it or not, a lot of people care who you are because you control their money. Overnight, you become very interesting to many people.

This results in phone calls and voicemails.
A ton of them.

I hated listening to my voicemails.

"You have . . . 17 new voicemails," my phone would constantly say. There were always voicemails.

So I'd grab a pen and paper.
And then I'd whimper.

Hi, Brad—or is it Bradley? Anyway, this is Gus from C-Tops-R-Us and I wanted to . . .

Hi, Mr. Hartmann. Was wondering if you received the bloated informational packet I dropped off . . .

Hi, Bradley—or is it Brad? Hoping I can get 20 minutes of your time to talk shower rods with you . . .

Every now and then this drivel would be punctuated by something funny, clever, or unique:

I'll be quick and to the point because I know you get 17 new voicemails every hour from people you don't know. And no, you don't know me either. Not yet anyway. Five years from now, after we've been kicking ass, taking names, and helping you get promoted to a VP role in Hawaii, you'll remember this day as the day you first heard from me. And my name is . . . (click)

Call over.
The caller hung up.

Huh?
Who was that?

Now I'm interested.
Very interested.

A curiosity gap was opened, and I need to close it.
I yell at a coworker to come in and listen to this thing.

We take bets on who it was.

It was probably the highlight of my day.
Maybe the week.

Now I can't wait to talk to this wild man and see what his deal is. Literally.

Now . . . will this tactic work for everyone?
No.

But the lesson is simple: Get creative. Think of what your voicemail will sound like on the other end of the line.

Use the voice recorder on your smartphone to record a few of your own voicemails. Play them back to someone else and have him or her grade them A+ through F.

Be memorable.
Be insightful.
Be funny.

Be something other than forgettable.

Open a curiosity gap and inspire your prospect to want to close it.

SHOW ME THE FAT
& SKINNY PHOTOS

As you ponder what specific pieces of value to deliver to your hot prospect, imagine you're pitching the latest and greatest fad diet program.

Seriously.

Fair or not, this analogy may be quite accurate from the perspective of the purchasing manager.

Embrace it.
Think like the team over at Beachbody.

Never heard of Beachbody? Stop reading and check out beachbody.com right now.

(Don't worry . . . I'll wait.)

Now, what do they do to persuade their customers?

They let their customers decide for themselves based on the results of other individuals . . . just like you. They show their customers their future. Their potential. They sell their message (and their product) by allowing current customers to show pictures of the undesirable state they were in and how much better they felt after using Beachbody's product.

Your challenge is to do the same with your prospects. Show them the before and after scenarios—that is, the fat and skinny photos.

Before working with your company:
unhealthy and unhappy.

After working with your company: fit, healthy, and lovin' life.

A good way to do this is with a specific written testimonial. Have your best client write a rave review based on your hard work. Then incorporate that into your marketing material.

How many clients can you call right now and request a glowing (and truthful) testimonial?

If it's fewer than five, make a 90-day goal to change it.

RULE 1.12

MAKE A MOVIE

A good way to demonstrate your fat/skinny credibility is with a client movie—a video testimonial. Have your best client describe your hard work on camera.

Salesmen are often reluctant to ask for this type of favor because the client relationship isn't strong enough. If this describes the majority of your business relationships, do something about it.

An even better way to show your fat/skinny photos is through the same video testimonial—but one from a client who is also a trusted friend of your prospect.

This shouldn't be that difficult if you've already invested your time in Rule 1.6: "Link Up. Link in." (on page 20). You should have found some indirect connections in your network to that of your prospect.

Someone who loves you who is also a friend of your prospect. These are the clients to target.

Most salesmen don't do this because of the fear of rejection. They aren't sure if the relationship is strong enough.

Then the excuses start.

- *Where would we film?*
- *What if there's bad lighting?*
- *Who owns a good video camera?*
- *Do I have to buy any equipment?*
- *Who will produce and edit it?*
- *Do we need any software?*

And then someone suggests that a written testimonial is nearly as good. And thus you continue down the path to mediocrity.

Specific, relevant, and memorable successes from current clients—told in their own words—is the most powerful sales tool you can have. Unless, of course, your client is willing to reach out to your prospects and make the call for you . . .

Don't gasp, it happens more often than you think.

When was the last time it happened to you?

BONUS

FORGET YOUR FAX

Junk your fax machine.
That revolution is over.

The minute you ask for my fax number, I immediately lose a bit of respect for you.

Fax machines are outdated.

They run out of paper.
And when there *is* paper, it inevitably jams.

They run out of ink.
The phone lines get busy.
They get disconnected.

Fax machines become another BS reason something didn't get done.

If you need a fax machine to do business with your partners, fine. Just don't use it when you do business with me.

Ideally, I don't even know you own one.

Buy a scanner.
Use email to send documents.

If there's a situation where a fax machine is more efficient than email, I have yet to hear of it.

Forget your fax.

MASTERING THE MEETING

n Part II—Mastering the Meeting—we will review techniques to help you make a great impression at your initial meeting. Using tips from Part I, you've gotten your prospect's attention—now et's nail the face-to-face meeting.

RULE 2.1

DON'T SEND A BOY

When the Hartmann family gets together, one thing is certain: there will be gambling—most likely of the Texas Hold 'em variety. During these activities (which, inevitably, bring out the worst in us), one line is guaranteed to be uttered no fewer than once every three minutes.

"Don't send a boy."

My father has been saying it for as long as I've been gambling, and in the Hartmann family, we start 'em young.

The cliché means you better not send a boy to do a man's job. It means, you better bring out the big guns. It means, if you're gonna kill the king, you better not miss.

It means . . . it's probably just a bluff.

When I repurposed this phrase for purchasing, however, it was no bluff. I meant it.

Don't send a boy.

I want a single point of contact with the power (perceived or otherwise) to get things done. If we're talking numbers, I don't want you to phone-a-friend, nor do I want to play the car-salesman game where you say, *"Let me talk to my manager . . . I'll be right back."*

Don't send a boy.

Inevitably, things will go wrong.

When they do, my single point of contact better be able to lead us to a solution. Quickly.

If this can never happen in your company because it's small and bureaucratic and privately held and the 90-year-old founder is still making every decision from his dark socks and sandals in Naples . . .
I don't care.

Make it appear that I have one point of contact who has the power to get things done.

Don't send a boy.

RULE 2.2

DON'T SEND AN ARMY

Don't send an army.

When we have a meeting, please do not bring seven employees with you. I'm not that important, and your colleagues have other things to do.

"You know Kramer in Sales . . .
"And this is his boss Jerry, from Corporate . . .
"And this is Lomez our regional IT guy . . .
"And this is Elaine, in Accounting . . .
"And this is George, the Assistant to the Traveling Secretary . . . "

Stop.
Please stop.
I'm sure they're all nice people, but I don't care.

I want one human who can get things done.

If this one person needs to memorize your 3-D org chart in order to get things done, fine. Keep it behind closed doors.

Yours.

Bringing an army of people just to meet with me is ridiculous. It makes me question the bureaucracy, redundancy, and inefficiencies in your company that will end up costing me time and money.

So don't send a boy.
But don't send an army either.

RULE 2.3

ACE "THE QUESTION"

When meeting with sales reps for the first time, I always pose the same question.

Every time.
Same question.

Despite the fact I knew these salesmen had been trained to answer this question intelligently, at least six out of ten replied with some unremarkable, obtuse response.

This was my question:

"Why are you different?"

Oddly, this query still caught most by surprise.
And the knee-jerk responses were always the same.

Great people.
Great service.
Wide selection.

Quick turnaround.
Good prices.

Uh . . . and great people.

So I'd say, *"No one ever says they have jerks working for them and we're a production builder so we buy a very narrow selection of products. Everyone delivers next day . . . "*

Pause.
I let the awkward silence sink in . . .

"So that brings us to price. If you don't have any true differentiation from my current supplier, your prices better be amazing. Are they?"

Maybe my expectations were too high.
Or maybe I was being an asshole.

From my perspective, if you couldn't clearly identify your differentiation and why it was of value to me, you were wasting my time. Get out.

If you have no additional elements of value to discuss, you must want to focus purely on price.

OK, fine.
Let's do that.

The most legendary response I ever received from *"Why are you different?"* was this:

"Uhh, well, I don't know. I don't know what my competition is doing or how we compare. You just need to trust us . . . Just give us a shot and you'll see how we are different."

I asked if he might be able to foreshadow this unknowable differentiation I may find after agreeing to partner with him.

"Honestly, I don't know how we'll be different. But you'll be happy with us, I guarantee it."

The meeting was over three minutes later.

"Why are you different?" is the distant cousin to the interview question, *"How many gas stations are there in the United States?"* The actual response is less important than the quality of thinking that goes on behind it.

For example, if I were to ask *"Why are you different?"* you can say, *"Our people."*

If you truly believe your staff is better, provide me with some proof.

"I'm glad you asked, Bradley. We believe our people are the best in the business. To test that hypothesis, we identified 43 salespeople in our market from five different competitors and we found our staff has, on average, five more years experience in the industry. Furthermore, our team averages 16 years with our company. We hire great people and they don't leave."

I may or may not choose to believe this, but the answer is thoughtful and intelligent.

So be prepared: *How are you different?*

RULE 2.4

GENERICIZE

If you are struggling with the *"Why are you different?"* question, read the classic *Harvard Business Review* article by Micheal Treacy and Fred Wiersema titled, *"Customer Intimacy and Other Value Disciplines."*[13]

The authors identify three generic value disciplines, or "three paths to market leadership."

1. Operational Excellence
2. Customer Intimacy
3. Product Leadership

Operational Excellence is all about reducing unnecessary overhead and redundancy in an effort to deliver the lowest price with the most convenience.

For Operational Excellence, think FedEx and Walmart.

Customer Intimacy, unsurprisingly, is about

---

13. Micheal Treacy and Fred Wiersema, *"Customer Intimacy and Other Value Disciplines,"* *Harvard Business Review*, January-February, 1993, pp. 84-93.

committing completely to the customer. Companies focusing on Customer Intimacy establish their processes and procedures around customer satisfaction. Companies in this space can slice and dice the market, segmenting the focus on the customers who are willing to pay more for great customer service.

For Customer Intimacy, think Nordstrom.

Companies that choose Product Leadership "strive to produce a continuous stream of state-of-the-art products and services," according to Treacy and Wiersema. It's all about Innovation.

For Product Leadership, think Apple.

Treacy and Wiersema note that when you choose a Value Discipline, you are, in effect, choosing customers too. There's a reason you don't typically see Bentleys in Walmart parking lots.

Different customers.
Different standards.
Different expectations.

If you are thinking, *Hmm, I think we are Operationally Excellent and Intimate with our Customers.*

Doubtful.
It's more likely you are neither than both.

Regardless, your company should agree on which Value Discipline it pursues.

If nothing else, it will allow you to answer, *"Why are you different?"*

RULE 2.5

ILLUMINATE AN INSIGHT

Experience is overrated.
I'll prove it to you.

My grandfather is 94. Since he was about 12 months old, he's been walking upright. On two feet.

He's a more experienced walker than I am by about 60 years.

Is he a better walker?

No.

Does he know more about walking?

No.

Can he teach someone else how to walk better than I can?

No.

As Rich Horwath, founder of the Strategic Thinking Institute, says, *"Experience, without expertise, means nothing."*

"Unless we're actively generating insights about our businesses, we're simply not taking full advantage of our experience. Insights are the bridge from experience to expertise . . ."[14]

Skip the part about your extensive experience.
Show me the insights.

Tell me a small nugget of truth about your business that will change the way I look at my business.

Do you actively generate new business insights?
Do you catalog your new business insights?
Do you share your new business insights with your teammates?

If you answered NO to any of these questions, read *Deep Dive* by Rich Horwath immediately. In his book, Horwath discusses the fundamentals of strategic thinking which, in turn, drive business insights.

Skip the experience.
Show me the insights.

---

14. strategyskills.com/are-you-insightful-or-insight-less

RULE 2.6

KEEP IT SIMPLE, SMARTIE

During my first week in the Purchasing Department at Pulte Homes, I called all my vendors and set up meetings to get myself up to speed.

The purpose of each meeting was this: in 30 minutes, I'm looking to get the high-level information about *Me* and *You*.

Me
What do I need to know about my new role?
How have we done things in the past?
How should we do them in the future?

I wanted to understand my vendors' perspectives on pricing, product, quantities, data management, outstanding POs—anything and everything.

You
What are you really good at?
How are we making your life easier?

How are we slowing you down?
How can we work together better?
What's happening in the next 12 months regarding prices?

The first meeting was with a flooring contractor.
It was brutal.

The flooring backup was a mathematical Chernobyl.
It was Excel on acid. Formulas were linked together
on multiple pages, but some of the pages were
gone. Many numbers were hard-typed, rendering
formulas worthless.

No one knew why we were paying what we were paying.
The vendor only knew it wasn't enough.

So starting with vinyl flooring, I asked what the detail
(i.e., the math) should look like.

"How can we make this easy?" I asked.

The explanation I received was anything but easy.
It sounded as if we needed MIT data scientists
to develop algorithms for accurate vinyl-flooring
installation procedures.

Apparently, to accurately price vinyl material and
labor several advanced degrees were necessary.

It seemed as if the strategy was to confuse me.
Maybe it was?

Ten minutes later I called the meeting to a close.
No wonder the backup was a mess.
Everything was far too complicated.

I asked the vendor to come back in two weeks with
a functioning Excel template based on our most
popular floorplan.

"Keep it simple and be prepared to explain it to me like I'm an 8-year-old," I said.

The next meeting was with our mirrors, shower doors, and accessories installer.

The vendor's owner walks in.

"We won't need 30 minutes," he says, dropping a three-ring binder on the table. *"We have a handful of products, we give you great pricing, and we bend over backward to make you happy. Here's a breakdown of the products we are installing in each community with the unit pricing . . .*

"We have some outstanding POs, but overall everything is OK. We'll make your life easy when it comes to this stuff. Worry about the bigger accounts. And if things go the way they have been . . . you'll hand this account off to someone else in six months.

"Now . . . what else can we do for you?"

The owner wasn't trying to impress me with all the BS he has to deal with. He didn't mention anything about importing from China or boxcars full of octagon-shaped mirrors.

He gave me the info I needed, had a sense of humor, and left. Brilliant.

Don't overcomplicate things.

Don't try to blow my mind with all the challenges involved in your business. I don't want to run your business; I just need to understand it so I can run mine.

RULE 2.7

FLY LIKE A CANDOR

Jack Welch, former CEO of GE, called candor the biggest secret in business.

We all want to be treated with candor.
We all want the unvarnished truth.

Are you prepared to ask for it?

Don't be afraid to ask direct questions. If you believe I will base my selection solely on lowest price . . . ask.

"Will you ultimately choose based on the lowest price?"

Ask the question.
You may just get an honest answer.

A salesman sitting across from my desk once asked, *"My goal is to win your business and start helping you build homes. Do you think I'm in a good position to do that in the next three months?"*

I could see he was nervous.

His hands were shaking.
His voice cracked a bit.

I shot him straight.

*"The business is yours to lose at this point, but
you won't be working on our jobs for close to nine
months. We've got several other priorities that take
precedence . . ."*

That was the truth.

Another time I was asked, *"If you could change one
thing about the millwork contract, what would it be?"*

I said, *"About once a week for the past 12 months I get
a call from some superintendent asking why he has 12
extra sticks of base left over after the trim carpenter
leaves. Solve this problem and I may award you the
business on that alone."*

Ask the questions you want answered.
You may hear the truth.

BE H.I.P.

H.I.P.

Humorous.
Insightful.
Passionate.

A surprising number of salesmen fail to conceal the contempt they have for their job.

They are not H.I.P.

There is no humor.
There is no insight.
There is no passion.

If you are 0 for 3 on the H.I.P. counter, you are done. No sales for you.

You get a sticker that reads, *"Hi. My name is Willy Loman."* Put it on your forehead.

H is for Humor

A rep from a supplier in Minnesota called me one morning. Said he was only in town for the day and would love to meet with me.

"If you agree to meet with me for five minutes—only five minutes!—I promise to bring you the best meatball sandwich you've ever had."

"What?" I replied, dumbfounded.

"I dunno, man. I just wanted to say something to get your attention. Can I get 5 minutes? I'll set the timer on my watch as soon as I see you . . . "

Out of curiosity, I agreed to meet him. He was a young kid, no more than 24. He wasn't obese, but he was certainly . . . chunky. He was disheveled. His dark, curly hair was short and unkempt. It was like he road a motorcycle to meet me.

His appearance alone was amusing. He was the type of person you'd think of later and chuckle to yourself.

And he had a meatball sandwich.
It was 4 pm.

"As you can tell, I love meatball sandwiches. Thanks for seeing me."

We met for 20 minutes and his sales pitch consisted mostly of jokes. He admitted that his prices were average and that his products were commodities, but he said I should give him a shot because I'd love working with him. He said that he was awesome. And he was. As were several other things he talked about, including my meatball sandwich. Awesome.

After he left, I felt the urge to work with him simply for his humor alone. He was funny.

Not that being funny is the sole reason to select a vendor, but I know of worse reasons.

This isn't Syria.
It's dimensional lumber.

The ability to make work fun and enjoyable is an advantage.

I is for Insights.
In Rule 2.5: "Illuminate an Insight," (on page 51) we talked about insights.

We won't beat this over your head . . . just make sure you have *some* business insights.

P is for Passion.
When it comes to passion, the playing field is made of carpet. I've met several carpet sales reps who truly loved carpet. Truly.

Not even Daniel Day Lewis could pull this kind of act off. These guys *really* loved talking carpet.

Cut piles.
Woven fibers.
Stain resistant vs. stain proof.
Carpet made from recycled water bottles.
Padding made from recycled car seats.
Virgin petrochemical resources.
Textured plush.
Berber.
Shag.

These guys could go on all day.
And they would if you'd let them.

They exuded so much passion I'd go home and find
myself repeating the history of Dalton, Georgia,[15]
to my wife. Their passion for carpets was literally
infectious. After meeting with them I was sick with
Everstrand® technology or CrushResister® nylon. I
couldn't stop thinking about it—it was a viral infection.

Passion is admirable.

H = Humor
I = Insights
P = Passion

You don't necessarily need all three.
The H.I.P. triple crown is hard to come by.

At the minimum, though, you need to commit to at
least one. Working with a solid pair is obviously better.

As a salesperson, rate yourself on the three H.I.P.
pillars through the eyes of the purchasing manager.
Better yet, have your teammates rate you.

Be honest with what you see.

Then honestly go about improving your degree of H.I.P.

---

15. Just as Cooperstown, New York, is home to the Baseball Hall of Fame, Dalton,
    Georgia, is the Carpet Hall of Fame.

RULE 2.9

QUIT WAVING THE GUN AROUND

PowerPoint is like a gun.
Quit waving it around.

If you're going to show me a PowerPoint, make sure
you know how to use it—and make sure it doesn't
suck. If you're unsure if your PowerPoint sucks or not
. . . it probably does.

Let me help you.
Read these two books.

1. *HBR Guide to Persuasive Presentations,*
by Nancy Duarte[16]

This is a Harvard production, so, unsurprisingly, it's more
of a left-brain view of the presentation process: a logical
and systematic breakdown from beginning to end.

---

16. duarte.com/book/hbr-guide-to-persuasive-presentations

2. *Presentation Zen,* by Garr Reynolds[17]

This is a right-brain, creative evaluation of slide-deck development. With numerous examples of slides that illustrate the good and the bad of presentations, this book is designed to help you improve your presentation in minutes.

Read them.
Study them.
Share them.

Or avoid PowerPoint altogether.

17. presentationzen.com

RULE 2.10

ILLUSTRATE THE SUPPLY CHAIN

While at Pulte Homes, I managed 13 different account categories, including labor and materials, across six different markets.

This isn't meant to impress you; it's meant to impress *upon you* how challenging this is. It's damn near impossible to maintain any level of detail and accuracy without partners to help carry the load.

Like any endeavor, teamwork is critical to getting things done.

You are critically important to the success of any purchasing manager you work with.

Yeah . . . I know it doesn't feel that way too often, but that doesn't make it untrue.

Your business acumen and—most importantly—your ability to communicate that acumen helps get things done. For you and me both.

Take drywall, for example. I struggled to understand the market forces that made 1/2" drywall in Chicago significantly more expensive than it was in, say, Denver or Indianapolis.

I struggled to understand this because I didn't understand the drywall supply chain.

Where did the gypsum come from?
Literally . . . what mine did it come from?
What other raw materials are required?
How is it all transported?
How many intermediaries separate me from the manufacturer?

Around this time, my Indianapolis supplier invited me down to visit a gypsum quarry, tour the manufacturing plant, and learn the process involved in producing drywall.

Eight hours later, three things had changed:

1. I was significantly more intelligent on the subject of drywall.
2. I had a newfound respect for those in the drywall business because I witnessed firsthand the challenges involved in making it.
3. The supplier and I had strengthened our relationship.

Upon my return to the office, I went straight to work. I mapped out every drywall manufacturer in the country, pinpointed every active gypsum mine, identified the location of each power plant that produced synthetic gypsum, began tracking the commodity price of pulp, and detailed the most likely methods of transportation.

In short, I illustrated the drywall supply chain.

Then I labeled the prices we were paying in each market for 1/2", 5/8", fireboard and the rest of the lovable gypsum products.

Here's a universal fact: people don't like to admit that they are clueless about their jobs.

Yet frequently, purchasing managers become responsible for activities of which they know nothing about. You can bitch about it or you can leverage it to your benefit—and the benefit of your future client.

Save managers time and money by illustrating your supply chain. Simplify your business down to its essential components.

Invest a few hundred bucks and have a graphic designer make it look clean and professional.

Without creating a teacher-student scenario, ensure the purchasing manager has a good grasp of the fundamentals that determine why your products cost as much as they do.

Share how your company reduces overhead given the business constraints. Explain the questions every purchasing manager should ask someone in your business.

If you feel you cannot trust the purchasing manager with this information, don't do business with the company. It's that simple.

Otherwise, illustrate the supply chain and you'll impress your future client.

GIVE ME CONTEXT
OR GIVE ME DEATH

I once worked with a project manager who said, *"We are so busy right now, we can't even use a schedule. Just tell everyone to go as fast as they can wherever they can."*

I quit the next day.
(Different story for a different time.)

But sometimes that happens.
In Purchasing, the pace can be like that for six months at a clip.

Keep this in mind when it comes to new products.

When presenting new products, it's critical that you analyze the context first.

What am I working on?
What am I stressing out about?
Are there new jobs with pending deadlines?
Am I transitioning new trade partners on older jobs?

If you don't know . . . ask.
Find out.

If you are interested in talking about a new sink base cabinet with a plastic, mold-resistant floor when my superintendents constantly bitch about being short two sticks of scribe molding on every kitchen . . . I may be less than interested.

I'll tell you to solve the scribe issue and come back in 60 days.

But new products can make everyone look good and keep our customers excited about their purchases.

If you want to push a new product, do this first: *get feedback from my sales team.* (This should look familiar to you—Rule 1.8: "Swing By Sales," on page 26.)

Be smart here; not all salespeople are made equal. Find out which salespeople have the biggest impact.

Do not reach out to the VP of Sales—that's too high. That's not good for anyone.

Start at the local community level. Document the people you spoke with—when you spoke to them and what they said.

Assuming the feedback from the sales team is positive, talk to the superintendents.

What are the challenges in installing the product?

Is it easier to install or harder?
It is easier to break or harder?

Again, document this information well.
(See Rule 1.2: "Gordon Gekko's 2nd Principle," on page 12.)

Assuming the feedback from the supers is positive, now you can start thinking about pitching me.

Should this new product be standard or an option?
How would you price the option?
How many colors would you include?

What's your recommendation on a product rollout?
When should we phase in the new product?

You should establish a fully thought-out implementation plan.

But remember . . . *context.*

If sales is on board, the superintendents are in, and I'm not pulling my hair out, then go ahead . . . schedule the new-product chat.

RULE 2.12

DON'T GO MONO

A rep from a national siding company once left me a voicemail. He was flying in from the Southwest and wanted very much to meet me.

The rep was in town all day.
He was willing to meet wherever, whenever.
"Just pick a time," he said.

Meeting time comes, and I'm surprised to see two people. Main Guy and Main Guy Jr.
I was never introduced to Jr.

They sit down and the theater begins.

"Thanks for seeing us, Bradley—is it Brad or Bradley? Which do you prefer? I don't know about you, but I answer to anything. Ha! So let me tell you why I'm here. We've got this new vinyl siding . . ."

Fast-forward 16 minutes. He's still talking, but nearing the end of the presentation. I have not said one word.

Truth is, I don't think he wanted me to ask any questions. He was like the waiter who's so focused on spitting out the details of the soup du jour that he forgets it's not about him . . . or his specials.

It's about the customer.

Main Guy finishes.
Then Main Guy Jr. chimes in.

"So do you have any questions?"

Annoyed and bored by the rambling soliloquy, I have only one question.

"Do you know what we offer today in this market?"

"Uhhh, no," Main Guy answers. *"Great point. What do you offer?"* he asks, turning the tables.

And here is where I come to a crossroad.

I could be candid—and rude—and explain how I really feel . . .

I'm insulted by your 20,000-word monologue on the bright future of vinyl. If I wanted anything from you, it would simply be dialogue. I want conversations that revolve around solving my problems or saving me money. Or both, ideally.

You were so caught up in your own bullshit about stuff I don't care about that you never even considered how we're doing business today.

I could say that.
It would help them in the short run.
And in the long run.

But I don't.
I don't have the energy or the interest.

"Looks interesting, guys. I'll float this by the team at next week's meeting and we'll go from there. Thanks!"

They seem pleased.
Clueless, but pleased.

Here is the lesson: Unless I tell you otherwise, I want a conversation, not a lecture. I want a dialogue, not a pitch.

Ask intelligent questions to get me thinking, and then let's just talk.

Dialogue > Monologue.

When choosing between Monologue and Dialogue . . . don't go Mono.

BONUS

LEAVE ON TIME

If we agree to meet from 2:00 to 2:30, leave by 2:30 sharp.

Unless I beg you to stay.

You're not going to close the deal in one meeting anyway.

Being respectful of my time is a sign of good scheduling, self-control, and discipline. All excellent characteristics to have.

If I have to kick you out of my office, I'll make sure I don't put myself in that situation again.

NAVIGATING THE NEGOTIATION

You've gotten your prospect's attention and you've had a few successful meetings. Now you are engaged in the negotiation process.

In Part III—Navigating the Negotiation— you'll learn tips and techniques to impress your prospect to the point where partnering with you is the only logical outcome.

RULE 3.1

MAKE ME LOOK SMART

Mike was a general manager at a Midwest drywall supply company. One day he sent me a brief email.

"I get this stuff all the time. Thought you'd enjoy reading it."
—Mike

Along with this 12-word email, there was an attachment. It was a multipage analysis of the drywall industry conducted by people much smarter than I at JP Morgan Chase. It had charts and graphs and was loaded with relevant information.

It identified commodity-pricing trends currently impacting the drywall business. It detailed supply and demand across the country. It made predictions on future pricing.

This, I thought, could make me look smarter. Better yet, it could actually *make* me smarter.

So I read it.

I contacted Mike and asked him several questions. He gave me intelligent answers.

During internal Pulte meetings, I shared what I had learned and identified the source material, if not Mike's role in sharing the source material with me.

This transpired over the course of a few days, all of which happened to fall during the negotiations to award a single-source supplier of drywall.

As it turned out, Mike's company won the work.

Did Mike win the work solely because he shared the industry analysis?

Of course not.

Mike's existing customers, whom I contacted without his knowledge, all said they loved working with him. He also had fantastic pricing. What's more, he had already made myself and my company smarter by sharing the market analysis.

In short, he made the decision easy for us.

During negotiations, get creative with elements or resources at your disposal.

What information can you share that will help you be perceived as the industry expert?

Needless to say (but I'll say it anyway), always be ethical and truthful.

You're in this for the long run. Don't use short-term tactics that can turn into long-term liabilities.

NOTE A NEW IDEA
TO AN OLD PROBLEM

During a negotiation, don't fall into the trap of trying to narrow your focus too much. Sure, you may end up haggling over .02/linear foot of primed poplar shoe molding, but keep an eye on The Big Picture.

The purchasing manager is looking for solutions on multiple fronts. Your value can extend beyond the specific products and labor you provide.

Visit various jobsites and look for pain points.
Talk to people.

Think about the problems they are having.

If you have ideas that could help solve a problem, your prospect will be interested.

Rarely is there anything truly new in construction.

The most common problems are the ones that have been around for decades. If you can offer intelligent solutions to old problems that are a thorn in your prospect's side . . . you'll increase your value.

RULE 3.3

BE ADEQUATE AT EXCEL

Remember José Oquendo? The über-utility man for the St. Louis Cardinals in the early '90s?

Well, I do.

José Oquendo once played all nine positions in a single Major League Baseball game.

Microsoft Excel is a lot like José Oquendo—it can get the job done for any number of purchasing activities.

If you don't have Excel skills, find someone who does.

Or better yet, pay $25 a month and get proficient at Lynda.com.

Lynda.com is a training website where you can watch hundreds of online video tutorials that can teach you software and business skills and help you to be more creative.

It's unacceptable to send in your bid on the back of a bar napkin or some random document that is convenient for you.

If I send you an Excel spreadsheet to fill out . . . *do it.* Pretty please, with a cherry on top.

If you opt not to, it just makes more work for me.

If everyone uses the template I send out, that allows me to easily copy and paste multiple bids at once. If they don't . . . I have to input all the numbers by hand. This annoys me. Needless to say, annoying firms are rarely awarded new projects.

If you know of an easier way for me to compare the multiple bids arriving on my desk, fantastic, let's discuss it. Otherwise, just fill out the spreadsheet I send over.

RULE 3.4

TAP DANCE AROUND TRANSPARENCY

Like many companies, Pulte embraced *transparency* during the economic death spiral of 2007-08.

Transparency became an instant buzzword (and buzzkill). It was like *Kardashian* except that in addition to being ubiquitous, it could also take money out of your wallet.

From the homebuilder's viewpoint, transparency ensured we knew what we were buying and why. From the other side of the table, transparency was an Excel-based Svengali used to extract every last nickel of profit from every contract.

So how can you best handle the transparency demand?

Here are a few tips.

BE OPEN TO THE DISCUSSION.

Many trades reacted violently to the idea of complete transparency. As one owner told me, *"Fuck off. If you wanna know all the details of my business, then buy my company!"*

Unsurprisingly, I was not his biggest supporter thereafter. I understood his point, but I thought he could have handled the situation more appropriately.

Approach the situation as you would any demand from a prospect—with curiosity and professionalism.

ASK QUESTIONS—A LOT OF QUESTIONS.

We were sent a large, confusing spreadsheet with hundreds of inputs.

We received about 20 minutes of training on it and were sent forth to complete an in-depth analysis of each company—ideally with their full and willing participation.

Nearly every question was open to some interpretation.

What was their effective labor rate?
What was their estimated material pricing?
How much inventory did they keep?
What was the size of their fleet?
What was their admin headcount?

I could easily count the number of people and trucks, but I was less willing to inform the owner that, in my humble opinion, he should fire the secretary and sell three box trucks.

As purchasing managers, we weren't stupid, but we

weren't McKinsey & Company analysts either. Between the owner and me, I was fairly certain he knew more about his business than I did.

Many trade partners used this knowledge gap to their advantage. We were asking for water and they gave us the fire hose. They provided so much information we couldn't digest a fraction of it.

Eventually, time management and logic forced us to move onto something else.

BE CERTAIN YOU UNDERSTAND THE SPREADSHEET.

Again, ask a lot of questions.

Few managers understood how the entire spreadsheet worked. Most simply asked the trade partner to fill it out and hoped they did it well enough so they could pass it onto someone higher up the corporate food chain for analysis.

A long-time trade partner of mine asked if I could fully explain the spreadsheet to him.

"No, I can't." I said.

"Well, I'll show you whatever you want, but you gotta come to my office."

So my boss and my boss's boss went to the trade partner's office for a full day and looked over everything.

Open kimono.
Ten hours.

We left believing him when he said he was losing

money doing our work.

Then what?

We all agreed there was no way we could do this for every one of my accounts, let alone every trade partner in the Midwest.

So we all silently agreed to focus on more effective ways to run the business. That was it.

So what's the point?

Be candid.
Ask a lot of direct questions.

If you feel your profit margin is on the line, ask about it.

"What would you like my profit margin to be?"

If the answer is zero, then you know you don't want the business anyway.

Transparency can be used to strengthen your relationships with clients without ruining your company or your bottom line. Be open and honest and ask your customer to do the same.

RULE 3.5

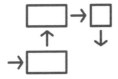

PROCESS MAP YOUR OPERATION

As organizations age, *work-arounds* develop organically.

You know what a work-around is, right?

It's the business equivalent of calling a plumber to fix your master-bath toilet only to watch him "solve" your problem by recommending you tinkle in the hall bath.

Employees with good intentions find new ways to work around problems without actually solving them. Over time, these inadvertent business processes consume time and money. Meanwhile, people don't actually understand why they are following these processes in the first place.

An intelligent first step is to process map your key customer-facing processes.

For example, your customer calls in requesting 12 more feet of crown molding. The delivery was short.

Starting with the in-bound phone call, map out each step on a whiteboard to understand the full scope of your operational response.

Include every step, procedure, and person involved. Do. Not. Skip. Anything.

Grab a marker, walk up to the whiteboard, and draw a single square. Write the first step in the process here.

Now draw another square next to it.
Write the second step of the process here.

If you arrive at a fork in the road, flesh out every single step in the process for each of the various scenarios.

Guaranteed you'll find some redundancy and duplication.

After you've streamlined and simplified the core operational services, have a graphic designer illustrate the process for your own internal-training purposes, as well as for proof of your business acumen.

I completed this exercise a number of times with several of my trade partners, and it was always eye opening for everyone. Complete the work ahead of time and use the results not only to simplify your business, but to win new business as well.

RULE 3.6

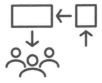

PROCESS MAP MY OPERATION

After you've organized your own corporate closet, you can then direct your attention to your prospect.

Again, start with curiosity.

If one of your superintendents requests that additional material be added to the contract, how would you like that process to be managed?

If we find an incorrect payment has been issued to us, how would you prefer we handle that with you?

As you document the answers with a process map, you may uncover ideas that can help your future client simplify his life—not to mention your own.

The process map process forces people to think.

Still not sure where to begin?

If someone says, *"We don't need to review this particular process. We've been doing it the same way for nine years."*

Start there.

RULE 3.7

DOCUMENT YOUR ASSUMPTIONS

Assumptions get a bad rap.

"When you assume, you make an *ASS* out of *U* and *ME."*

We've all heard that before, right?

But assumptions aren't all bad.

The assumptions you need to watch out for are the undocumented ones. In particular, the undocumented assumptions that remove money from your pocket. For example, here are a few assumptions you might make:

Assumption 1
If we ship the complete bill of materials that ties out correctly to our contract, the builder will not ask us to return to pick up additional materials at no cost.

Assumption 2
In the unlikely event that gas prices spike north of $5 per gallon, the builder will be willing to accept a gas surcharge to share in the commodity hike.

Assumption 3
If we find there were errors in the prints during the bidding process that result in a higher contract price, the builder won't ask us to eat the difference.

You get the idea.

When these events happen, you will quickly discover if the assumptions you made were harmless or not.

Don't do that.
Don't wait.

When both sides come prepared with their *Top 10 Assumptions* about the potential working relationship, untold hours can be saved.

It might not always be pleasant, but it's far better to complete this exercise early on than to make the assumptions and keep them undocumented.

If your assumptions turn out to be incorrect, you may not wish to have me as a partner. For more on this, see Rule 1.1: "Start with why," on page 10.

RULE 3.8

BE SMART WITH YOUR SAMPLES

Samples are sales tools. Use them to simplify the sales process, not to annoy your prospect.

First things first: When delivering samples, don't simply drop them off in the lobby with the secretary. This is an opportunity to make another positive connection with the person who can help deliver a YES.

Schedule a date and time to deliver the samples.

If I say, *"Just swing by and drop them off whenever you want . . . I'll get 'em,"* convince me that you want to make this decision as easy as possible for me, regardless of which direction I choose. In order to do so, you need to walk me through the specific samples, a few unique attributes, and the pricing.

Guarantee me it will take no more than seven minutes. Tell me that if it takes any longer, you'll donate $500 to George Costanza's *The Human Fund.*

And if your *Seinfeld* joke goes over his head, he'll think you're quite the humanitarian. No harm, no foul.

When the sample delivery meeting takes place, make a joke about the seven-minute timeframe and set your watch. Then make sure you're gone in six minutes.

Now that your samples have arrived, they should drive a decision. That's the reason for their existence.

Confirm the timetable for the decision. If no timetable is established, this is an opportunity to take a leadership role.

Ask questions for the lack of timeframe.

- *What is stopping you from making a decision?*
- *What other information do you still need?*
- *What other priorities are ahead of this decision?*
- *Beyond your approval, who else has a deciding vote in the decision?*

Hopefully you have this information prior to this stage, but if you don't—ask the question now.

Armed with this information, determine if your insight into the typical sales cycle of your product can be used to make the process easier for your prospect.

You've solved this problem before (customers evaluating your product against the competition); *can that information help here?*

Once the decision has been made, remove the samples.

Allow me to repeat: once the decision has been made, remove the samples.

If they sit around long enough, the purchasing team throws them in the garbage.

When that happens, you lose money (the samples), you lose another face-to-face opportunity (the pickup) and you annoy me (I have better things to do than to throw away your samples).

Be smart with your samples.

RULE 3.9

REMEMBER WHEN YOU SUCKED

The sales representative seemed genuinely puzzled.

I, in turn, was genuinely puzzled by his genuine puzzlement.

"That was eight years ago, Bradley. Everything has changed since then," he claimed. *"Almost all those people you remember . . . they're all gone. We've overhauled everything. We now have the best quality in the industry. Here, look at this article by the—"*

I didn't want to read the article.
I was lost in the memories of the past . . .

Years prior, I had been a trim superintendent, the construction manager responsible for completing the home after drywall. The purchasing team at the time had made a sweet little deal to save a few bucks by switching door-hardware manufacturers.

To the casual observer, the new hardware was the same as the old hardware. It looked similar, it felt similar, and it smelled similar.[18]

The only problem was, *it didn't do what it was supposed to do.* And hardware has a rather narrow set of performance expectations.

No, this new hardware was definitely not working . . .

Doors became locked when they were unlocked. (Think parents and babies . . . *not good.*)

Locked doors suddenly became unlocked. (Think parents and teenagers, or teenagers and parents . . . either way, *not good*.)

As the trim superintendent, it was my fault it happened and it was my responsibility to fix it.

Soon thereafter, I came to a conclusion: the hardware was shit. As an extension, my life went to shit when I had to deal with all the shit that came from dealing with the hardware shit.

(Yes, this period of my life still haunts me.)

This story of shit, near verbatim, was what I told the puzzled sales rep.

"Your company may have had a lot of turnover, but we haven't," I explained to him. *"A lot of people around here still remember what life was like dealing with your product. And it wasn't good."*

---

18. Yes, hardware has its own smell.

He stared at me.

"Even if you could offer incredible savings," I continued, *"how can I justify the target that will be on my back when I risk taking the company—my friends and co-workers—on another trip to hardware hell?"*

If we've purchased your product in the past ten years and it failed, start working on a detailed plan on brand building.

Read a book on Toyota—they've bounced back from customer fury.

Hire a consultant.

Book a PR firm.

Whatever you do, you better be really creative and really convincing. Your story better be like *Rudy, Hoosiers,* and *The Karate Kid* (the original one, with Elisabeth Shue) all rolled into one.

And you might as well hire Mr. Miyagi to sell the shit out of it.

It can be done.
Brands reemerge all the time.
But it won't be easy.

Don't expect me to go easy on you either.

RULE 3.10

REMEMBER, I WANT STARTERS

The guy was persistent, but likable. Every month, he'd plead for an opportunity to show me his great pricing and his amazing service.

"I know you don't have a need right now, but trust me—you'll love what we have to show you."

Fine.

The meeting went smoothly, and a few days later his quote arrived at my desk. His numbers were . . . *annoying*.

Across the board, on the entire bill of materials, he was 5 to 10 percent higher than my current pricing.

I called him. *"These are your best numbers? Really? This is why you were dogging me for six months?"*

"Well, no. Those aren't my best numbers, but I want to be your #2 guy. I want to build your bench strength.

When your current provider fails you, I'll be there, ready to go!"

I was pissed off.
Thanks, but no thanks.

Let *me* worry about my bench strength.
You should aim to be a starter whenever you get the chance.

If you want to win my business, then play your best hand and let the chips fall where they may. This supplier's stunt wasted my time (and his) and was counterproductive to his winning our business.

As it happened, several months later, our existing supplier did in fact fall down on the job. We decided to replace him.

I didn't even bid out Mr.-I-Want-To-Be-Your-#2.

Don't waste my time if your goal is simply to position yourself as the #2 guy.

I want starters, not a deeper bench.

RULE 3.11

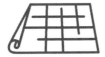

HELP SIMPLIFY MY PLANS

If we're being honest with each other, we've already acknowledged that the blueprints I have you bid from don't actually get built in the field.

Some version of them gets built, but there will be variation. The variation may be subtle, or it may be an alternate reality.

You know this.
I know this.

So let's work together.

We've covered the first step in this process (Rule 3.7: "Document Your Assumptions," on page 90). The next step is to help us simplify our blueprints.

Instead of simply taking orders based on what's on the prints (*"OK . . . 14 left-hand, hollow-core primed Colonial doors"*), ask us if we've considered changing sizes to improve the layout.

Ask us why we chose for some reason to have the hall bath door and the hall closet door potentially slamming into each other.

Based on your expertise, identify ways our floor plans could be improved. Even if we opt to ignore your advice, we'll appreciate the fact that you are looking for ways to improve the overall product, not just complete a takeoff.

Complete a takeoff and you're doing the minimum.

Identify improvements we can take company-wide and you become invaluable.

If you are concerned about diplomacy, complete the takeoff as is. Then include an appendix humbly titled, "Ideas to simplify and/or save money."

It will be read.

And if it isn't, you'll have a much better understanding of the type of people you are dealing with.

RULE 3.12

YES. YOU REALLY ARE 2% HIGH

My millwork supplier was frustrated.

"Man, Hartmann . . . " he sighed, *"you always tell me I'm 2 percent high. I think it's your way of haggling for a few extra bucks as we get close to the finish line."*

He may have verbalized his thought as a declarative sentence, but it was a question.

He wanted to know if this was a tactic of mine—to shave a few bucks off the bottom line. He wanted to know . . . if I was lying.

Here's what I told him . . .

"Dude. You are 2 percent high. Take that info and do whatever you like with it. If you don't want to change your number, then don't. We'll see what happens.

"But . . . if you can drop a few points and still be happy about winning the work, then I'd suggest you do that. To award this work, I need to persuade guys in Purchasing and Operations why I'm making my recommendation.

"It's always helpful when you're the low man or the next-to-lowest. That 2 percent I recommended to you, that will get you into the top-two conversation. But . . . do whatever you want."

He did drop the price.
He did win the work.

Would he have landed the work without it?
Maybe. It would have been close.

Here's the real question: Do some purchasing managers use this "You're 2 percent high" tactic with every contractor on every bid?

Yes, some do.

That's why I suggest calling a few bluffs every now and then. If you never call a bluff, you never get to see the cards.

Try it.

If Purchasing calls to share that you're 2 percent high, kindly inform them you put a lot of thought into the bid and are comfortable with where your numbers are—win, lose, or draw.

Don't budge.
See what happens.

BONUS

ASK ME IF YOU'RE DEAD

At some point during the negotiation process, you may get the distinct feeling that you're a dead man walking.

That you have no chance of winning the business.

If you get this feeling, ask if you are or not.
You may get a truthful answer.

During a three-company bid process, an owner called me a few days after bid submittal.

"Be honest now . . . do we have any chance of winning this thing? We tried our best, but I got the feeling we're out of this race. Am I right?"

He was right.
I told him so.

"I appreciate you telling me. We've got a few other good opportunities out there, and I want to focus our

efforts where we can win. Those other two guys will treat you right. Good luck."

Immediately, I had more respect for the owner.
And now both of us could use our time more efficiently.

If you think you're dead, just ask.
The only thing worse than being dead is not knowing it.

AMAZING YOUR ACCOUNT

You've attracted some attention, prepared well for the meetings, and won the negotiation. You've successfully earned new business. Congratulations.

However, landing the business and keeping it require different skill sets. In Part IV—Amazing Your Account—we'll review how to make sure you keep the business long-term.

RULE 4.1

BE THE B.O.M.

You must be the Master of your Domain.
The King of the Castle.
The Queen of the Realm.

Simply put, you must own the Bill of Materials supporting your contracts. I don't care if the purchasing manager gave you the list of products for the base house with strict orders not to question his all-knowing brilliance . . .

You must own the Bill of Materials.
They are yours.

Once you accept that and act upon it consistently, your value to your builder clients will increase by a factor of 17.[19]

Every line item on every spreadsheet for every model home in every community is *your* responsibility.

---

19. Yes. I made this figure up, but it's around 17, give or take a few.

I can hire any company to ship out the materials on a list. The companies that differentiate themselves ensure they know what's on every single base house and option, why it's there, and have considered alternatives to doing the work more efficiently.

If it sounds like a lot of work and responsibility, it is.

That's why most don't do it.

DWYSYAGTD

It's pronounced (dwiss-ee-AHG-tee-dee).

A strange series of letters that separates the pros from the schmos.

Do
What
You
Say
You
Are
Going
To
Do

It's that simple.

If you're not going to do it, don't say you are.

Frequently, I would have excited outside-sales reps

leave my office promising to deliver things (quotes, samples, ideas, etc.) the very next day.

I'd let them know I wouldn't have time to review whatever they sent me until the following week, but it was their choice.

"Send it whenever you can next week," I'd say.

"That's OK, no problem," they'd reply. *"I'll get you this stuff tomorrow."*

Fair enough.

If that was the promise, I'd make a note in my calendar to look for the information the following day.

When the info failed to arrive the next day, I'd send an email.

"That info you promised to deliver yesterday . . . Can I expect it today?"

A surprisingly large percentage of the time, the answer was no.

"Oh. You said you weren't going to look at it until next week."

Oh sure . . . my fault. I'd think. *If this guy would turn the tables on me here, 24 hours after the meeting, what will be my fault 24 months from now?*

It was a stupid way to lose credibility, although not uncommon.

Say what you mean.
Mean what you say.

Under-promise and over-deliver.

DWYSYAGTD:

Do
What
You
Say
You
Are
Going
To
Do

RULE 4.3

HAPPY SUPERS MAKE ME HAPPY

Superintendents deal with a lot of garbage—literally and figuratively.

Crazy homeowners, for one.

Then there are the numerous suppliers, the dozens of trade contractors, the municipal-building inspectors, the merciless OSHA inspectors, and on and on . . .

Then, of course, there are the salespeople who care about one thing: *their closing date*
(read: their commission).

And that's just the obvious stuff.
(I won't even bring up the Army Corps of Engineers . . .)

When I change a contractor or supplier, this places an additional piano-like burden on the backs of the superintendents, who must retrain the newbies how the jobsite rolls.

So remember: *happy superintendents make me happy.*

Bring *them* donuts.
Buy *them* pizza.
Give *them* NFL tickets.

Keep *them* happy.

After sufficiently satiating your supers, encourage them to let me know directly how much they love you.

Leverage *their* happiness in the field to influence *me* in the office. Trade partners and suppliers who are loved get more work.

If you don't have an organization chart of all our superintendents listed by jobsite, including cell numbers and email addresses, create one yourself.

Or just ask for one.

Happy superintendents make me happy.

RULE 4.4

BE MY EYES AND EARS
ON THE JOB

Purchasing managers are office monkeys.

They hang in the office all day and rarely get out to
the field.

You might think that purchasing managers visit the
field frequently to ensure that what they bought on
paper is actually being built in the home.

You'd be wrong.

In Purchasing, there is a never-ending list of things to do:

Updating existing contracts.
Pricing out new floorplans.
Pricing out new options.
Bidding out new communities.

And the obligatory gauntlet of daily meetings.

Jobsite visits for a purchasing manager are like movie nights for married couples with kids. Sure, you should make time for more of them, but you always end up staying home cleaning up other people's messes.

So what does this mean for you?

You can help improve our jobsite blindness.
You can help purchasing managers be in two places at once.

When visiting the field, what information can you share with the Purchasing team to keep them up to date?

Leaving your Purchasing contact rambling voicemails filled with information you witnessed on the job is better than nothing, but not very helpful.

Take pictures with your phone.

Record video of work in progress.

Snap some selfies with excess material along with ideas to eliminate it.

While in the field taking care of my superintendents (see Rule 4.3: "Happy Supers Make Me Happy," on page 113), use some of that technology in your phone to share your insights on how we can improve our product—or, better yet, reduce our house cost.

Be my eyes and ears on the job and you'll be top of mind.

RULE 4.5

LEVERAGE MANUFACTURERS

When preparing for battle, evaluate your strongest allies.

We've already discussed manufacturers in Rule 2.10: "Illustrate the Supply Chain" (on page 64). Boarding this train of thought, consider which manufacturers are geographically close to your operations and how they can help you differentiate and win business.

For example, a door manufacturer owned a small plant located ten miles from our office. I had grown up around that area yet had no idea the plant existed.

The manufacturer scheduled a plant tour with a box lunch for a few builders. We toured the site and learned about their latest innovations.

We learned about the massive tooling machines required to create aluminum exterior doors. We learned about the process required to create a 5/0 hollow-core interior door.

The tour was fascinating. My team learned several ways to mitigate issues we were having in the field.

I had a newfound respect for door manufacturers—and door suppliers. More importantly, by the time I left the plant, I was smarter.

That was my personal win.

In this case, the suppliers and manufacturers already had our business. The education they provided improved our team and strengthened our relationship.

What experience can you offer your clients that will change the way they view their world?

Consider your location and your most innovative manufacturers—where will your next plant tour be?

RULE 4.6

EMBRACE THE Z.D.I.

Tell me if this sounds familiar.

Your customer, for whom you bend over backward, calls to inform you she's switching to another vendor.

She appreciates your hard work, but . . . you lost the account.

You think, *Those ungrateful bastards, do they even realize all the work we did for them free of charge?*

Let me answer that for you: *No.*

All those second and third trips to Harrington Glen you did without complaint—or an additional invoice?

The superintendent never told anyone in Purchasing.

And that time you replaced all that stolen cabinetry free of charge after the home wasn't locked up at night?

The project manager kept a lid on that one.

Toot your own horn.
No one else will do it for you.

*So what's the best way to ensure Purchasing is aware
of all the additional work you do free of charge?*

The almighty Z.D.I.
The Zero Dollar Invoice.

Just send a standard invoice with agreed-upon
pricing, but with a full discount at the bottom.

For example, a four-hour round-trip box truck with two
employees to pick up extra materials.

Man hours = 8 x $35/hour = $280
Fuel charge = $120
Restocking fee = $100
Total Charge = $500

Hartmann Homes Discount = $500

Net balance = $0

PS: You're welcome.

Z.D.I.s help in two critical ways:

ONE
They inform the purchasing manager what's happening
in the field and how you're "partnering" consistently.

TWO
You are creating a paper trail for future evaluation
within your own company. If your Hartmann Homes

Z.D.I.s add up to $150K at the end of the year, you may want to reconsider your interest in their business.

Purchasing managers don't know all you do for them. Here are three reasons why:

ONE
Communication is often poor between Purchasing in the office and Construction in the field—two different sub-cultures, two different perspectives on the business.

TWO
When mistakes are made in the field, it's in the best interest of the mistake makers to keep the embarrassment local. No one wants to be made an example of.

THREE
You don't tell them.

I'd frequently have conversations with subs and suppliers about performance and they'd say, *"Well, what about a 'Thank You' for bailing the Madison Lakes team out of that flooring jam they were in?"*

I'd respond, *"Madison Lakes flooring jam? I have no idea what you are talking about . . ."*

Don't be a martyr. Just send a Z.D.I.—a Zero Dollar Invoice—when you perform activities you feel you should be paid for.

I pleaded with my subs and suppliers to send me Z.D.I.s so I knew what was happening in the field.

Few ever did.

Those who eventually lost my business wished they had.

RULE 4.7

READ TO LEAD

One of the easiest ways to stay in touch (without being annoying) is by passing on valuable information.

When you come across a relevant article in a trade magazine or the *Wall Street Journal*, cut it out and mail it along with a brief, handwritten note, *"Read this and thought you'd enjoy it."*

That's it.

Everyone likes to be top of mind in someplace other than their own.

Doing this via email works also, just not as effectively.

Go analog.
Use snail mail.
It means more.

The topic can be about leadership, management,

innovation, new products, time management, personal development—as long as the article is a good read and relevant . . . pass it along.

Here are a few of my favorite sources for content to share:

Magazines:
- *Fast Company*
- *Inc.*
- *Wired*
- *Harvard Business Review*
- *Sports Illustrated*

Online:
- LinkedIn
- the *Wall Street Journal*
- the *New York Times*

Individual Blogs:
- Ryan Holiday[20]
- Seth Godin[21]
- Shane Parrish[22]
- Chris Voss[23]

Twitter[24] is also a great way to sort through dozens of potential articles in seconds.

Even if it was an article everyone read, it's still a nice gesture that will likely be remembered.

Do this once per quarter and you'll be known as someone who is thoughtful and who stays current on trends in the industry.

---

20. ryanholiday.net/blog
21. sethgodin.com
22. fs.blog
23. blog.blackswanltd.com/the-edge
24. twitter.com

RULE 4.8

CALL ON THE BIG FISH

In *The New Strategic Selling*, the fantastic book by sales-strategy company Miller Heiman, authors Robert Miller and Stephen Heiman discuss the idea of "like-rank" selling.

When a first-year sales rep calls on the president of a company, there will inherently be some tension on the part of the newbie.

President the BIG fish.
Newbie the little fish.

This is where like-rank selling comes in.

Employees of the same rank in different organizations are kin. They are fighting the same fight. They share the same challenges, the same fears, the same victories.

Therefore, there is no inherent tension when they are asked to call on one another.

Why would there be?

They are on the same level.

GMs can call on other GMs.
VPs can call on other VPs.
Presidents can call on other presidents.

So what?

So you can use this same concept of like-selling also.
Or you can use this same concept in reverse.

Have your company's president, whose name happens
to be on the building, drop a quick line to the 26-year-
old purchasing manager.

Have him express how excited he is to work with the
builder. Have him say these exact words, *"Now . . . if
you ever need anything at all, don't hesitate to contact
me directly."*

Guess what the purchasing manager will feel?

Tension.
Surprise.
Excitement.
Honor.

In short, he'll feel important.

The purchasing manager will feel like the BIG fish.

People want to work with others who make them feel
important, like the BIG fish.

So, when strategizing about closing your next
prospect, don't forget about the BIG fish who has an
office 20 feet away from you.

RULE 4.9

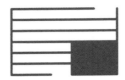

LEARN THE
FRANCIS UNDERWOOD PRINCIPLE

Francis Underwood, the ruthless character played by Kevin Spacey in the Netflix series *House of Cards*, has a mantra for leading politicos.

Vote your conscience and don't surprise me.

Underwood employs any number of tactics (intimidation, duplicity, murder, etc.) to "persuade" those unlucky enough to reside in his circle of influence.

However, he respects the fact that every politician's number-one job is reelection. You can choose to vote against Team Underwood, but stand your ground and let him know.

Ahead of time.

Surprises make people look bad.

Vote your conscience and don't surprise me.

As a purchasing manager, I had my own mantra when it came to pricing. It was simple.

Shoot me straight and don't surprise me.

First, your pricing always needs to be reasonable. Whatever that means for whatever you're selling.

It needs to be in the ballpark.
It needs to be around the dish.

It needs to withstand some logical questions as to how it came to be. That's it.

Then tell me what you need and what you want.
Price according to your conscience.
Shoot me straight.

Support your price quote with enough information so I can ask some intelligent questions. Then let's have a candid conversation.

That lump-sum quote you scribbled on a sheet of yellow pad paper? No good.

Separate material from labor.

Be prepared to tell me how much overhead and profit are included. Rough percentages will be fine.

Shoot me straight.

Then . . . *don't surprise me.*

If you know prices will rise, share this information as soon as possible.

My best suppliers and subcontractors informed me

about what was coming, encouraged me to budget for the increase, and laid out a plan describing how we would still get the best price on the street.

You're the expert.
I expect you to know what is happening with prices.

If we can anticipate price increases, it gives us more options to offset them. It allows my boss to forecast accordingly so that when the price does blow up, everyone is prepared.

And that's a good thing—for both of us.

When it comes to pricing, *shoot me straight and don't surprise me.*

Otherwise you may be exposed to some *Underwoodian* tactics of persuasion.

RULE 4.10

LEARN THE
BEN HARPER PRINCIPLE

And it hurts me
To look into the mirror at myself.
And it hurts even more
To have to be with somebody else.
And it's so hard to do,
And so easy to say.
But sometimes
Sometimes you just have to walk away.
Walk away . . .

—Ben Harper :: Walk Away[25]

If you're not familiar with singer-songwriter Ben Harper, check him out.[26] He's a talented musician and a great writer.

---

25. Credits: Ben Harper
26. benharper.com

His song "Walk Away" is probably a bit too emo for the general construction crowd, but that's too bad because I like it.

And here's why you should, too (at least for this analogy).

In what I like to call the Ben Harper Principle, the rule is simple: *if you merely pass along price increases without any ideas to offset them, I will walk away.*[27]

That's it.

Someone who simply passes along increases with a BS form letter from a manufacturer, shrugs and says, *"This is what they told me, so this is what I am telling you . . . "* isn't interested in keeping my business.

Individuals who do this are in the commodity business.
Individuals who do this are not thinking.
Individuals who do this are lazy.

If you simply pass on information—and materials—from one place to the next, you are adding no value.

You're the pharmacist in the Jerry Seinfeld joke—simply taking pills from a big bottle and putting them into a little bottle.

Stop and think.

Look at your business and consider ways we can offset the rising costs. Visit my jobsite and do the same.

Hell, I don't care if the ideas don't even involve your products!

---

27. OK, maybe not today, but trust me . . . I will start looking and bolt at the earliest opportunity that is most beneficial to me.

If you supply lumber and see an opportunity to save time and money in the paint activity, *tell me!*

Offset your price increases with ideas.

Remember the Ben Harper Principle: *if you merely pass along price increases without any ideas to offset them, I will walk away.*

RULE 4.11

CONNECT LIKE GLADWELL

In *The Tipping Point*, author Malcolm Gladwell offers his view on how ideas spread. It's a good read.

Gladwell applies the 80/20 Principle[28] to the spread of ideas; 20 percent of the people will do 80 percent of the work.

Gladwell dissects this 20-percent go-getter group. The first among them are the *Connectors. Connectors* know a lot of people and actively look to connect individuals in their network to everyone's benefit.

Connectors make a habit of introductions.

You want to be a *Connector*.

---

28. Also known as the Pareto Principle for you smarty-pants with good memories of business school.

Here is the easiest way to do this: Invite to lunch two purchasing managers from two different client firms.[29] Open the conversation by saying that you think the two of them would mutually benefit from meeting each other. Ask a few open-ended questions to get the conversation going and then get out of the way.

Being a *Connector* has enormous advantages.

First, since you've already won the business, this free lunch will be perceived as selfless—a perfect adjective for the salesperson you want to be.

Second, there's no downside. Worst-case scenario has two clients eating free food. Best case, these guys hit it off and will forever remember *you* as their *Connector*.

---

29. Needless to say, make sure these two people have something in common other than their day job. If they are both diehard Metallica fans . . . good enough. If one is 75 and hard of hearing and the other is a recent college grad with a texting addiction . . . probably not good enough.

RULE 4.12

CHOOSE CHANGE
OVER IRRELEVANCE

"If you don't like change, you're going to like irrelevance even less."

—General Eric Shinseki, retired Chief of Staff, U.S. Army

Chances are good your contact in Purchasing won't be in that job 18 months from now.

Maybe he'll get promoted.
Maybe he'll get fired.
Maybe he'll decide to become an actor.

Prepare for this change.

Meet the employees above him.
Meet the employees below him.
Map out the org chart.

Then prepare for the day he informs you he's leaving. Start preparing now.

He may or may not say it, but the new replacement will get no training.[30] You better have a plan to bring him up to speed right quick.

If you arrive on Day One of the new guy's reign and hand him a 12-page report with everything he needs to know, you'll be quickly added to the "Do NOT remove" list.

Include the following:
- *Current pricing by floor plan and community*
- *Current product listing by floor plan and community*
- *Ideas for improvement*
- *Threats that could make his life hell*
- *Outstanding invoices*

Prepare for this change or face irrelevance.

---

30. His training will largely consist of insurance indemnification and encouragement to separate labor from material.

BONUS

THE LAST WORD ON PRICING

If we're not making any money, then we're doing all this for practice. So let's close with a final note on pricing.

If you have the lowest price, *congratulations*! That will certainly help you win business, but it's no guarantee.

Especially in the long run. In case you weren't aware, construction folks gossip like schoolgirls. If your dedication and service isn't there, the building community will know about it. Quickly.

If you have the highest price, by definition you're not even in the ballpark. You're in the parking lot next door.

That's what you need to know about pricing.

If you are consistently delivering all sorts of unique value to your customers and prospects—like the ones specifically mentioned in this book—pricing doesn't matter that much.

You're not a commodity.
You're different.

The challenge is to consistently demonstrate your differentiation. That's why you've made it to the end of this book.

Companies have made billions differentiating water sold in plastic bottles. If they can do it with water, you can surely do it with whatever you're slinging.

Choose to be different.
Purchasing managers everywhere are pulling for you.

And make no mistake—they will still talk about you behind your back. But if you study the lists in this book and try some of these ideas, chances are when purchasing managers do talk about you, they'll be talking about how great you are to work with.

Now get out there and try some of these ideas.

NOW WHAT?

If you've found this book to be valuable and are wondering if there are other ways the Behind Your Back Sales Co. can help you, you're in luck. We offer several services customized for the LBM industry:

Consulting: Our consulting services are designed for LBM dealers, distributors, and manufacturers who are frustrated with challenges in their business. Partnering together, we help design the solution and ensure it's implemented intelligently to energize your employees and deliver value to your customers.

Coaching: We work with executive leaders, sales managers, and high potential employees to improve critical skills, including: leadership, personal productivity, time management (personal, team), sales team accountability, the craft of selling, public speaking, and presentation design.

Workshops: The Behind Your Back Sales Co. workshops are interactive training sessions customized specifically for your team. Our half-day, full-day, or two-day sessions include discussions, exercises, training tools, and custom workbooks.

Keynote: Bradley has been honored to speak at well over one hundred events across the U.S., to large audiences of 1500+ as well as small, private teams of executive leaders. Regardless of audience size or venue, he loves being able to connect and interact with attendees—getting them to engage, laugh, and, ultimately, commit to do something different as managers and leaders.

To learn more about these services, visit
behindyourbacksales.com

PRAISE FOR THE BEHIND YOUR BACK SALES COMPANY

"Bradley sees the world in a way most don't and his style is unorthodox to a purpose: he brings superior insights, an intriguing and entertaining communication style, and an offbeat (yet very professional) use of humor to business challenges."

— Ian Heller :: President at Modern Distribution Management

"If you haven't seen Bradley Hartmann... he's a truth slayer. We need more guys like him in the industry. He tells you like it is. I highly recommend him."

— Joel Fleischman :: CEO at Drexel Building Supply

"The common theme at our meeting was that it was our best meeting ever because we had Bradley Hartmann speaking. Changing sales behavior in salespeople is very hard to do. There is no doubt in my mind that Bradley and his message reached our team and influenced how they will interact with their customers in the future. That is always what we are striving for in these meetings, but it is rarely achieved."

— Craig Bradshaw :: President at Mead Lumber Company

FURTHER READING

Outliers, by Malcolm Gladwell

Made to Stick: Why Some Ideas Survive and Others Die, by Chip and Dan Heath

Presentation Zen, by Garr Reynolds

HBR Guide to Persuasive Presentations, by Nancy Duarte

To Sell is Human, by Daniel H. Pink

The New Strategic Selling, by Stephen E. Heiman, Diane Sanchez with Tad Tuleja

The Art of Profitability, Adrian Slywotzky

The Little Red Book of Selling, by Jeffrey Gitomer

Deep Dive: The Proven Method for Building Strategy, Focusing Your Resources, and *Taking Smart Action*, by Rich Horwath

Purple Cow: Transform Your Business by Being Remarkable, by Seth Godin

Ctrl Alt Delete: Reboot Your Business. Reboot Your Life. Your Future Depends on It., by Mitch Joel

Rework, by Jason Fried & David Heinemeier Hansson

The Little Book of Talent: 52 Tips for Improving Your Skills, by Daniel Coyle

Anything You Want, by Derek Sivers

ACKNOWLEDGMENTS

I'd like to thank my teammates, colleagues, and friends for generously sharing their hard-fought wisdom with me over the years, including Andrew Cooper, Arnie Harris, Bill Heuer, Bob Cave, Bob Horton, Chuck Chippero, Chuck Hager, Craig Stempowski, Dane Bix, Dan Sauser, Dave Sporina, Ed Dowdy, Eric Bates, Geoff Gran, Jason Herb, Jason Fischer, Jason Sabo, Jeff Lear, Jerry Rhodes, Joel Robinson, John Pohodich, Justin Benzel, Justin Fedora, Keith Miller, Kemp Gillis, Ken Raupp, Lantz Rakow, Leah Drake, Mark Seigle, Mark Vogelsberg, Matthew Schmidt, Mike Brown, Mike Hausler, Mike Rhoads, Mike Wahl, Nathan Marsh, Paul Schmit, Rich Horwath, Ron Rose, Ryan Stensland, Santa DeLeon, Sonia Svec, Tom Blancett and Walt Nashert.

Gracias to Jason Hines for his cover art and the entire set of BYB icons. Special thanks to Drew Holzfeind for his detailed and candid editing of this book.

Thanks to my siblings, Ann, Jeff, and Abby, and to my parents, Joyce and Scott, for their love and support. Most of all, thanks to my boys, Brayden and Redding, and to my wife, Melissa, who made this all possible.

ABOUT THE AUTHOR

BRADLEY HARTMANN is the founder and president of the Behind Your Back Sales Co. In his role as president, Hartmann works with LBM dealers, distributors, and manufacturers helping them create high-performance sales cultures by understanding what "the other side of the desk" is thinking and how they prefer to buy.

Hartmann was born into the lumber business. The son of an LBM manager, Bradley began working in lumber yards at the age of 14, chasing customers' trucks around the yard, re-stacking bunks of 2x4s, and occasionally racing the forklifts.

Throughout high school and college, Bradley worked in various segments of the LBM industry. Upon graduating from the University of Illinois with a degree in Spanish, Hartmann was hired by national homebuilder Pulte Homes.

Beginning in customer service, Bradley spent 8 years in the field, progressing from superintendent to project manager to area manager. He then transitioned into an area purchasing role, buying material and labor in seven midwestern markets from Ohio to Colorado. He enjoyed his years at Pulte and earned an MBA along the way.

In 2011, Hartmann launched his training and consulting firm to help lumber and building material companies eliminate the frustration, confusion, stress, and lost time associated with selling to builders.

As president, Hartmann's core services include consulting on marketing and selling to national homebuilders, helping sales managers and general managers drive incremental sales, Behind Your Back workshops for sales professionals, negotiation training workshops for leaders at all levels, and keynote speeches.

Hartmann has written six books for the industry, publishes *The Behind Your Back Newsletter*, and teaches at the university level. His podcast, *The Behind Your Back Podcast*, featuring industry thought leaders, is listened to by thousands of business leaders each month. Hartmann lives in Dallas, Texas, with his wife and two sons.

Made in United States
Orlando, FL
17 February 2022

14890418R00083